Original title:
Meaning of Life: Package Not Included

Copyright © 2025 Creative Arts Management OÜ
All rights reserved.

Author: Jude Lancaster
ISBN HARDBACK: 978-1-80566-058-3
ISBN PAPERBACK: 978-1-80566-353-9

## Epiphanies in Silence

In the quiet, I once found,
A sock and a note that was browned.
The wisdom of chaos, I swear,
Came wrapped in a twist of my hair.

The cat stared with knowing delight,
As I pondered what's wrong or right.
The toaster beeped like a sage,
Maybe I'm just stuck in a cage.

## The Art of Unraveled Truths


Life's puzzle, it seems I misplaced,
With corners that never quite faced.
I bought it in a thrift store, they said,
Turns out it was just someone's bed.

There's wisdom in crumbs from my snack,
Insights popping like cheese from a crack.
Unraveled truths from the fridge,
Maybe my fridge is a knowledge bridge.

## The Unwrapped Paradox

I unwrapped a gift filled with air,
Was the present just a big dare?
The tag read, 'open with glee',
But all that came was a bee.

I pondered my choice with a shrug,
Sipped on a cup, oh so snug.
The paradox danced in my mind,
As I searched for the grace I can't find.

## Empty Box, Endless Possibilities

An empty box, oh what a thrill,
It surely can't sit still!
A house for dreams or a hat for a cat,
Just imagine the fun that is at.

With each second, ideas take flight,
Could it be a rocket or a light?
In the void, I find my delight,
An empty box feels just right.

## Labyrinths of Thoughts and Feelings

In the maze of my mind,
Thoughts race around and unwind,
Like a hamster on wheels,
Spinning truths that conceal.

I ponder my socks' missing mate,
Was it a plot or just fate?
Each question leads to a grin,
As my sanity starts to thin.

Feelings dance like jellybeans,
In a quirky line of routines,
Do they mean what they say?
Or are they just here to play?

So I wander through this jest,
Searching for what feels like the best,
Only to trip on a thought,
Hey, I forgot what I sought!

## The Enigma of Yesterday

Yesterday waved with a smile,
Teasing me all the while,
Did I trip over my plans,
Or dance with invisible fans?

The wisdoms of yore confuse,
I laugh at the paths I choose,
Did I really eat that whole pie?
Or just ask my dreams to fly?

Memories float like balloons,
Tangled in old silly tunes,
Each note is a clever riddle,
Woven through life's quirky fiddle.

So I juggle with time's playful tricks,
Mixing up yesterday's flicks,
In the theater of my cheer,
Where the past draws too near!

## **The Dance of Dust and Dreams**

Dust bunnies waltz on the floor,
Chasing dreams, they suddenly soar,
What if they find a new place,
To join in the cosmic race?

In the corners, the sunlight gleams,
Chasing shadows of old schemes,
Do dreams get tired from the grind,
Or just play hide and seek, unkind?

I twirl with the scent of old books,
Wishing for curious looks,
As I trip on ambition's glee,
Dust tumbles and laughs at me!

So let's dance with dust and fate,
In a rhythm that feels first-rate,
Where every step's a delight,
Giggling through the silent night!

## Cracks in the Facade of Certainty

Certainty wore a fancy hat,
But slipped on a curious cat,
Each thought it wedged in the seams,
Burst forth with the wildest dreams.

Was it a cake or a mirage?
The wisdom felt like camouflage,
Questions poking through the crust,
Who knew certainty turned to dust?

I walk on this quirky tightrope,
Wobbling between folly and hope,
Each crack a reason to laugh,
At life's perplexing autograph.

So let the jester wear the crown,
In this wacky, upside-down town,
With a smile, I chase the sublime,
As certainty runs out of time!

## Musings in the Twilight of Time

In the twilight, shadows dance,
Questions swirl in a quirky trance.
Did I leave the oven on again?
Or should I ponder existential zen?

Cats plot world domination schemes,
While I trip over my wildest dreams.
Life's a riddle wrapped in a jest,
Where laughter's truly the very best.

## A Basket Without a Bottom

I carried a basket, full of my woes,
But it slipped through, as life often goes.
Running after, I stumbled and laughed,
Chasing dreams that are whimsically daft.

The more I grasp, the less I find,
Life's a puzzle designed to unwind.
With socks that don't match, and hair askew,
I chuckle at plans being utterly askew.

## The Conundrum of Choices

Choices loom large, like a buffet,
Do I want sprinkles or just a parfait?
A bit of this, and a dash of that,
Life's menu changes, it's quite the spat.

Left or right? Oh, what a mess!
Each decision's just a playful guess.
In the end, we laugh and delight,
Who knew indecision could be so light?

## Silent Stories Beneath the Surface

Beneath my calm facade, waves collide,
With tales of whimsy I struggle to hide.
An octopus in a top hat winks,
As I ponder over coffee and drinks.

Silent stories in each line I draw,
Who knew life could be so full of awe?
Leaves rustle secrets in a gentle breeze,
As I chase after nonsense with wondrous ease.

# The Canvas of Experience

Brush strokes of laughter, quirks on display,
Each splatter of paint leads us astray.
Yet in every mistake, a masterpiece lies,
Life's colorful chaos, a joyful surprise.

From spills on the floor to trips on our feet,
We twirl through the mess, looking for sweet.
Who knew that the blunders could bring us such cheer?
A canvas of moments, let's give a loud cheer!

## Shadows of Intent

Intentions as shadows play tricks in the light,
Chasing their tails, what a curious sight.
The plans that we make often lead us astray,
Like socks in the dryer, they vanish away.

We stumble and fumble, oh what a grand show,
Life's not straight lines, but a wiggly flow.
With laughter and joy, we dance through the dark,
For shadows can't catch us when we add a spark!

## Embracing the Unknown

Around the corner, the unknown awaits,
In a monster disguise or a box full of mates.
We leap into nonsense, with giggles galore,
Finding treasure in places we never explored.

Who knows what's ahead? Could be cake or a frog,
Or perhaps a wise sage, or a playful dog.
So we chuckle and grin as we take the big jump,
For life's just a circus; let's waltz with the clump!

## The Fabric of Reality

A quilt stitched with days, some frayed at the seams,
With patterns of dreams and outlandish schemes.
Each patch tells a story, some silly, some bold,
Woven with wisdom, a handful of gold.

Caution, dear friends, for it might unravel,
As we skip through the fabric, let's giggle and travel.
For in this grand tapestry, wild threads intertwine,
What's quirky and funny makes living divine!

# Echoes of a Mysterious Message

In a box marked 'fragile', the label is torn,
Swirling thoughts like confetti, my patience is worn.
I check for instructions, but none can be found,
Just echoes of laughter from the skies all around.

With a twist and a turn, I follow the sound,
Chasing shadows of wisdom that please me confound.
Every riddle I solve, leaves ten more in the dust,
A dance of confusion, oh, what a must!

## Navigating the Maze of Moments

I bought a GPS, but it's lost in the fray,
It leads me in circles, then shouts, 'Have a nice day!'
Each corner I turn brings a grin to my face,
As I stumble through life like a whimsical race.

A detour to happiness, or so it would seem,
Finding joy in the wrong way: what a marvelous dream!
With each puzzled step, I might trip up or fall,
But laughter is hidden in every dark hall.

## A Puzzle with Missing Pieces

I've got a grand puzzle with pieces galore,
But half of them vanished, oh what a chore!
I search high and low, through the sofa and chair,
And find that the answer was hiding in air.

With colors so bright, but shapes don't align,
I laugh as I build it, calling it 'divine'.
Each piece that I find, just adds to the fun,
What's missing? Oh dear, I guess that's my pun!

## The Quest for Uncharted Meanings

I packed up my bag with no map in my hand,
Set off on a journey to the whimsical land.
Where questions are plenty, and answers are few,
I giggle at hints that are cryptic, it's true.

The compass is spinning, a whirligig show,
I'm lost in the laughter; where do I go?
Every twist, every turn brings a smile to my face,
On this quest for the things that are hard to embrace.

## A Canvas with No Instructions

Blank canvas, colors fly,
Brushes dance, oh me, oh my.
No guidebook to show the way,
I'll splash and giggle, come what may.

Splatters here, a smear of blue,
What's this shape? A bird? A shoe?
I'll paint the sun as a purple sphere,
And laugh as my friends all cheer.

A masterpiece in every mess,
With jelly beans, I can't confess.
My palette's wild, no rules to heed,
Artistic chaos, yes indeed!

So here I stand, a joyful knight,
In a world where wrong feels right.
No labels, just a laugh or two,
A canvas full of me and you.

## The Art of Navigating Absence

Lost my keys, oh what a fate,
Tripped on shoes, can't find a mate.
Where's my mind? It wanders free,
In a landscape of absurdity.

Searching high, searching low,
In the fridge? No, that can't be so!
My socks are missing, what a plight,
They've eloped, oh what a sight!

Navigating absence like a pro,
With a map drawn in crayon flow.
I chart my course through empty space,
In the land of lost, I find my grace.

Laughter bubbles in this void,
Where wasted time is joy employed.
In every gap, a giggle waits,
Life's playful jest, my heart appreciates.

## Fragments of an Unscripted Tale

Once upon a time, I thought,
Life had a plot, or so I sought.
But every page is out of sync,
My storyline? A kitchen sink!

Characters with hats too tall,
Dropped the ball at the grand ball.
Plot twists wrapped in bubblegum,
And punchlines that go kaboom! What fun!

Each chapter's like a riddle wrapped,
In a world where logic's napped.
I scribble notes, then lose my pen,
Only to find it in my den.

So here's to tales with no clear end,
To laughter shared with every friend.
We'll write it loud, we'll write it free,
In this wild play, just you and me.

## The Silent Echo of Existence

In the quiet, echoes tease,
Thoughts drift by on a gentle breeze.
I ponder life and where I stand,
With mismatched socks and jelly in hand.

Whispers swirl, what's it all mean?
Do I nap or chase my dream?
With cups of tea, I'll take a seat,
This silent echo sounds quite sweet.

Dances of dust on sunlit rays,
Life's a circus, oh what a maze!
Laughing clowns and cotton candy,
With laughter bright, oh how dandy!

So let's embrace this crazy ride,
With joy and whimsy as our guide.
In the silence, let laughter ring,
For life's a song and we're the swing!

## Bridges over Uncrossed Waters

A bridge made of spaghetti wide,
Yet no sauce on the side.
We dance on noodles, oh so slick,
But who knew forks could do the trick?

With boats made of banana peels,
We sail on dreams that spin like reels.
Each paddle's just a gumdrop sweet,
While gummy fish call us to eat!

## The Journal of Unwritten Pages

A journal blank, so pure and bright,
Filled with doodles of snacks all night.
In margins, sticky notes do thrive,
Reminders to dance and take a dive!

Each page a wish, a laugh, a sigh,
With crayons drawn to make us fly.
But wait! An eraser rolled away,
Now everything's a grand ballet!

## **Windows to Untold Narratives**

A window cracked, a breeze so bold,
Peeking through to stories told.
Where cats wear hats and mice hold reins,
In worlds where chocolate flows like rains!

The sun is a disco ball up high,
While squirrels wear sunglasses, oh my!
We sip on milkshakes made of stars,
And race our dreams in candy cars!

## The Untold Chapters of Existence

In the chapters where socks go lost,
A kingdom ruled by lint, at cost.
They gather knights, all mismatched pairs,
To hold court in your favorite chairs!

The plot twist? A sneeze unveils,
An epic quest through sneezy trails.
With tissues flying, laughter loud,
We toast to chaos, proud and bowed!

## In Search of the Invisible Thread

With a map made of cotton candy,
I wandered through the whacky woods.
Each signpost said 'keep on laughing,'
I guess that's why I'm in these hoods.

A squirrel gave me life advice,
His acorns held the key to cheer.
I asked him, 'Got wisdom to slice?'
He grinned and offered me a beer.

In a world where socks go missing,
I chased the laundry's mighty curse.
Each sock that fled left me wishing,
For stories wrapped in a universe.

So here I am, with giggles high,
In search of threads that make us whole.
Invisible fortune but oh my,
It's just the laughs that fill my soul.

## The Hidden Treasures of Now

In the fridge, I found a pickle,
It waved at me from jar's embrace.
'This is treasure,' I began to giggle,
As it danced in the garlic space.

I strolled through dreams that never ripened,
With shoes too large for grown-up feet.
Barefoot joy, no longer frightened,
A life that's silly and quite sweet.

The clock sometimes winks, it's a prank,
Saying 'time's treasure is now, old chap!'
So I flipped it the bird, gave it a crank,
And napped on my groovy map.

From living for tomorrow's chance,
I learned the art of silly sway.
The hidden treasures of a dance,
Are moments that won't go away.

## Shadows of a Flickering Flame


A candle lit, it winked and blinked,
With shadows swirling, oh so sly.
I asked, 'Are you my thoughts in sync?'
It just chuckled and said, 'Try.'

The snacks I burned, a marshmallow fate,
Kept whispers of laughter in the night.
"Don't take life so serious, mate!"
Said the smoke as it took flight.

I wrestled thoughts like playful cats,
Chasing ideas that come and go.
In the dim, I wore my silly hats,
And let my giggles steal the show.

Shadows dance on the wall of jest,
They remind me life is absurd.
In the flickers, I find my zest,
More than wisdom, we're simply stirred.

## Weaving Stories from Ashes

I found some ashes on a plate,
Once a campfire, now tiny dust.
I thought, 'Is this my fate?
Or just my recipes gone bust?'

Piecing together burnt memories,
With a pinch of salt and a laugh.
Each error turns to funny stories,
Cooking up joy in every half.

So I crafted tales from charred remains,
Of marshmallows that flew to the stars.
And whispered secrets on the trains,
Of goofy dreams and silly jars.

In the ashes, laughter blooms slow,
As wisdom stumbles on the floor.
Life's a quilt, stitched high and low,
With stories, I'm never a bore.

## Starlit Wanderings

Under the stars, I stumble and roam,
Searching for answers far from home.
A squirrel whispers secrets in the night,
But I'm still puzzled, try as I might.

In the darkness, I trip on my shoe,
This cosmic quest feels like a zoo.
I laugh with the moon, it chuckles back,
While I spin in circles, what do I lack?

The breeze carries giggles, a playful tease,
As I ponder life like a child with ease.
Falling over thoughts, I grace the ground,
In the great scheme, what have I found?

A dance with the stars, a twirl of chance,
With each slip and slide, I'll laugh and prance.
Though questions linger, my heart feels light,
In this silly journey, I take flight.

## **The Unseen Compass**

With a compass missing its very needle,
I navigate life like an off-key fiddle.
Maps confuse me, I'll take the back roads,
Plot twist! I swapped 'em for quirky codes.

Turn left at the humor, right at the fun,
Voices of mirth, everyone's on the run.
I stop for directions, a llama appears,
Says follow your dreams, but bring lots of beers!

Life's got its quirks, like a buttered toast,
You grip it just right, and it might just coast.
But flip it upside down, it's chaos anew,
Every adventure, a laugh when it's due.

rough the twists of the night and the bumps of the day,
With friends by my side, we'll laugh all the way.
Though lost every time, I'll smile while I roam,
In this fab journey, I find my way home.

**Beyond the Surface**

Beneath the surface, where the water's still,
Fish are gossiping, they've got time to kill.
They murmur of dreams in their splashing pool,
But I'm just a human, what a funny duel!

I ask a turtle, "What's life all about?"
It shrugs in response, "Still working it out."
A starfish laughs, says, "Just go with the flow,
While seaweed dances, put on quite a show!"

Floating on waves, I ponder the sea,
Who knew deep thoughts could come from a bee?
Jellyfish jive while I sip my drink,
Maybe it's better not to overthink!

So here in this world, where the currents sway,
I'll keep laughing, dancing, come what may.
Each ripple and wave brings a chuckle, a cheer,
Life's quirky moments, the thing that I hold dear.

## Infinite Inquiries

Why do socks vanish, why is the sky blue?
Why do we question things that we can't view?
I ponder it all on a lazy old chair,
While my cat curls beside me, without a care.

Each thought that bounces is another odd query,
Like why does my hair always seem so dreary?
I'll ask every coffee mug, every plate,
But they just sit silent, it's quite a fate!

I write down my madness, the answers unfold,
Like a tapestry blooming, in colors so bold.
I laugh at the chaos, the answers too vague,
Like trying to catch the wind with a paste of old plague!

So I'll dance through the questions, embrace all the fun,
In the carnival of life, there's still much to run.
With each silly query, a smile appears wide,
In this land of the quirky, I'll take it in stride.

## The Gift of the Unfathomable

Oh, the box that's labeled 'surprise',
Inside there's socks and a pair of pies.
We unwrap the joys, the quirks we find,
Is that a pet rock? It's one of a kind.

We search for wisdom in cookie crumbs,
While asking questions like, "Why do we hum?"
The manual's missing, that's quite bizarre,
But laughter's the compass, guiding us far.

In this treasure chest with no user guide,
Who knew a goldfish could turn the tide?
We dance with hope, we jiggle with glee,
Life's a jest, just let it be free.

So here's to the gifts that make us grin,
To chaos and laughter, let the fun begin!
We'll toast our whims with quirky delight,
In this gift of chaos, life feels so right.

## Embracing the Unwritten Chapter

Life's an open book, but where's the plot?
Are we the heroes? Or just a robot?
Each page we turn, a new twist in sight,
Is that a chicken? Oh what a plight!

We scribble our dreams in crayon-fed lists,
Ignoring the chapters our future insists.
The words seem jumbled, like pasta on walls,
But sometimes the laughter is worth all the falls.

Plot twist! The dog has taken the stage,
He howls a soliloquy from his cage.
We're just sidekicks in this crazy show,
Life's best punchlines, they steal the flow.

So let's jump ahead and make it our own,
With scribbles and giggles, our hearts have grown.
We write our tales in the wackiest ways,
In this unwritten script, we'll spend our days.

## Potpourri of Dreams and Realities

In a blender of thoughts, we toss our dreams,
Add a sprinkle of chaos, or so it seems.
A dash of reality, a hint of surprise,
Is that the pizza? Oh my, such pies!

We mix our wishes with marshmallow fluff,
Life's recipe calls for just enough stuff.
A little of this and a pinch of that,
Who's in the kitchen? The cat's gone flat!

A whiff of adventure, a scoop of delight,
We bake up the laughter that's out of sight.
What's cooking today? Oh, just fear and fun,
With every mishap, a new day begun.

So gather your dreams, your moments absurd,
Life serves a potpourri with laughter as word.
Taste every flavor, let your heart sing,
In this dish of existence, we're all chefs in spring.

## A Symphony of Uncertainty


Picture a concert of clams and cats,
With cymbals of chaos and turtle hats.
We conduct the weirdness with baton in hand,
Is that a kazoo? Oh, isn't it grand?

The notes are all jumbled, a pizza surprise,
As we harmonize laughter through googly eyes.
The bass has taken off; it danced with the drums,
The solo? A sneeze, and then it hums!

Each player's a mess, but what a delight,
In the chaos of sound, we find pure light.
We're swirling in rhythms that tickle our feet,
In this symphony wild, life's endlessly sweet.

So here's to the music, the laughter we share,
With every odd note, we move without care.
Life's strange concerto, we joyfully play,
In this symphony dizzy, we'll dance the day away.

## Lighthouses on a Foggy Shore

In misty fog where lighthouses blink,
A seagull scoffs, says, "What do you think?"
Waves crash with whimsy, rocks shuffle and slide,
Who needs a map when you can just ride?

With every gust, a tale gets spun,
A sailor lost in laughter, not fun!
Waves whisper secrets, but the punchline stings,
Life's just a riddle made of silly things.

Battered boats bobbing, they tease the shore,
"Did you bring snacks?" they jest, wanting more.
"Your compass is broken!" the breeze likes to shout,
Yet around every corner, there's wiggle and doubt.

So dance with the tide, let joy find you there,
With lighthouses guiding through whimsical air.
And if you find reason, it's all in the jest,
Just laugh with the waves, and forget all the rest.

## The Paradox of Expectations

I wore my best shoes to the grand parade,
Dreamt of fanfare, maybe a charade.
But instead of glitz, I stumbled on gum,
With each grand plan, here comes the hum.

Expectation whispers, "You'll be the star!"
Yet I'm dodging chaos, oh what bizarre!
Life's like a jigsaw, with pieces misplaced,
Finding joy means staying quite well-faced.

I once thought wisdom was a treasure chest,
But it turns out, it's a comedy fest.
With every wrong turn, a laugh seems to bloom,
Life's not a rocket; it's more like a broom.

So here's to the mishaps and jumbled delight,
Where every misstep feels oddly so right.
Just brace for the tumble, don't fear the fall,
Because in this big circus, we all have a ball!

## Unfolding the Layers of Now

I peeled back the layers, like an onion did weep,
Search for the wisdom, but forgot how to sleep.
The layers keep coming, like cake at a feast,
With frosting of laughter and crumbs of the least.

What's at the center? Is it joy or a frown?
Each layer reveals why I'm all turned around.
Thought I'd find answers, but instead found a clown,
Wearing my jacket, yelling, "Wear joy as a crown!"

Peeling and stacking, it's rather grand,
Life's just a puzzle made out of sand.
The sun shines bright, yet I'm searching for shade,
In layers of laughter, my worries just fade.

So let's flip through the pages of this silly book,
With every dark turn, there's another fun hook.
And if you feel lost, just dance in the now,
The layers crumble softly beneath your brow.

**The Terrain of Impermanence**

In the land of hiccups, where moments take flight,
Time winks and chuckles, from morning till night.
With every small blunder, a kitesurfing fall,
You realize life's just a not-so-calm squall.

Cobwebs of yesterday drift quietly past,
While I search for wisdom that's fading so fast.
"Remember that time?" echoes through the air,
With giggles of ghosts who just don't seem to care.

Imperfect as ice cream on a hot summer's day,
Yet each melting moment, deliciously gay.
So grab onto laughter like it's all you've got,
In this goofy terrain, aim for the hot spot.

So let your heart wander, embrace the refrain,
For fortune and folly dance in the rain.
With every new twist, remember, it's true:
Life's a wobbly ride, and it's all up to you.

## Melodies from an Unplayed Tune

A song that's stuck inside my head,
With notes that dance but never tread.
The lyrics all are lost in time,
Yet I hum along, still feel sublime.

A symphony of awkward sounds,
In my own world, laughter abounds.
I search for meaning in the beat,
But end up tapping my two left feet.

A melody that won't be sung,
With harmonies that come undone.
I've mislaid the composer's chart,
But the fun begins where I depart.

So let the silence wrap its wings,
As I compose these foolish things.
The tune may fade; the joy won't cease,
For in the folly, I find my peace.

## The Illusion of Security

I bought a lock for peace of mind,
Yet left the key with one more find.
The door is locked, the window's cracked,
I still feel safe, but that's abstract.

In cozy corners of my home,
I hide from fears that tend to roam.
The cat's my guard, on every chair,
Yet she's just snoozing without a care.

Wrapped in blankets, in my nook,
I sip my tea, and read a book.
The world outside can spin and sway,
But I just laugh at the dismay.

So here I sit, a fortress bold,
In pajamas that defeat the cold.
With snacks and giggles lined in rows,
Who cares if danger ever shows?

## **Dreams Floating in Midair**

A dream once soared, then took a dive,
It landed hard, but still, I strive.
It flutters now like laundry pinned,
To hopes and wishes, a twisty wind.

I built a castle made of fluff,
With reality, it gets quite tough.
The clouds are nice, but seem to tease,
As I tumble down with grace and ease.

I chase my thoughts, they run away,
Yet giggles follow in the fray.
With silly plans and wild schemes,
Life's but a dance, or so it seems.

So I'll keep flying, though I fall,
In my balloon, I'll heed the call.
A whimsical plight, a sight so grand,
With dreams afloat, I'll make my stand.

## The Search for Hidden Clarity

I wandered through the fog with glee,
Searching for sense where none should be.
With each wrong turn, I cracked a grin,
For clarity is dense; it's built on spin.

I asked the trees for wise advice,
They whispered back, "Just roll the dice."
The wind just laughed, a cheeky breath,
And danced away to tease my quest.

With glasses on that weren't my own,
I peered through markets, thrifted, bone.
What's right or wrong? A playful game,
Who needs the prize when fun's the aim?

So here I am, in haze and cheer,
Enjoying riddles, far and near.
The more I seek to find my way,
The more I laugh at life's ballet.

## Questions without Labels

Why's the sky so blue, I ask,
While dreaming of a sunny flask.
Is it lemonade or just plain air?
I ponder while I twist my hair.

Why do socks go missing fast?
Perhaps they've found a future vast.
In strange dimensions where they sail,
While I'm left with one, it's a fail.

Do dogs have secret lives at night?
Planning heists beneath the moonlight?
They gather 'round with tails a-wag,
While I adjust my dinner swag.

Is the world a giant game to play?
With rules that change from day to day?
I laugh as I stumble through each ride,
In this wacky trip, I'll take in stride.

**Threads of Tomorrow**

What lies ahead in yarns of fate?
Will I weave a scarf or get a plate?
Maybe I'll knit a hat for a goose,
And make my life a quirky use.

Tomorrow's threads are bright but weird,
Like outfits made of dreams, I've steered.
Will my sweater unravel fast?
Or will it be a cozy blast?

I spin my doubts like fluffy clouds,
Mix patterns, frills, and even shrouds.
What if my future seems askew?
I'll just wear polka dots, how about you?

So here I sit, with needles ready,
Creating joy, a life not petty.
In every stitch, a laugh I find,
As I shape the dreams in my own mind.

## **Loose Ends Today**

Tangled thoughts on a sunny spree,
Like spaghetti flying from a bee.
Can you fix your hair with a fork?
Or discuss the weather while playing dork?

Loose ends trail behind like streamers,
Dancing in the breeze, oh such schemers!
Will my keys reappear on their own?
Or must I search amidst the foam?

What if I wear mismatched shoes?
Will the world giggle or just snooze?
In this kaleidoscope I prance,
With every misstep, life's a dance.

So here's to chaos all around,
In each moment, laughter's found.
Today's the day I'll raise a toast,
To life's oddities, let's make a boast!

## Adventures in the Unknown

What's behind that weird old door?
Could it lead to a dragon's lore?
Or just a room where gnomes reside,
With party hats and fish to hide?

I'll pack some snacks and take a leap,
Into a world where secrets creep.
Will I meet a wizard with a beard?
Or find a cat that's quite revered?

Navigating through the bizarre,
Is it just me or does time spar?
In "Alice in Wonderland" I gleam,
As I chase down an oddball dream.

Every corner hides a tale to tell,
Of whimsical things wrought with spell.
So off I go, with laughter's tune,
Into the unknown, beneath a moon.

## Footprints on Shifting Sands

On shifting sands, I stroll with glee,
Leave footprints that won't stay with me.
Will they dance away with each tide?
Or are they shy, wanting to hide?

Each grain, a story, each step a laugh,
Am I a traveler on a goofy path?
Chasing tumbleweeds and a wayward hat,
Shouting out "Where's my pet cat?"

The sun dips low, a melting dream,
As I ponder life's quirky theme.
What if my tailless prints are for naught?
In a world where confusion is all I've sought?

But here I stand, with arms out wide,
As waves wash in, I take the ride.
So here's to laughs in sights unseen,
On shifting sands, life's just like a screen.

## Dancing with the Unfamiliar

Twisting and twirling on this floor,
Every step feels like a chore.
With two left feet and a goofy grin,
I wonder where this dance will begin.

The music plays, my toes do tap,
Yet, I trip on thoughts that overlap.
The crowd looks on, some start to laugh,
As I shuffle off my awkward path.

Mirror balls glimmer above my head,
Reflecting dreams like crumbs of bread.
Life's dance partner, bold and spry,
Says, "Just have fun! Don't ask why!"

So I bowl over with charming grace,
In this waltz of a curious place.
If falling's a trick that life will reveal,
Let's laugh it off and dance with zeal!

## Reflections in a Broken Mirror

This mirror, cracked, shows me a face,
A patchwork of laughs in a jolly space.
My left eyebrow's raised, and the right one's shy,
I can't help but wonder, oh me, oh my!

I lean in close to have a peek,
How often do I laugh, or feel so bleak?
These shattered fragments, a colorful quilt,
A reminder that life's a hand-built tilt.

The reflection grins, "Embrace the mess!"
Says, "Chaos is just a grand party dress!"
So I dance with shards, every piece a jest,
Winking at fate, I'll try my best!

With every crack, there's a tale to tell,
In this funhouse mirror, all's well.
In silly distortions, I find delight,
My patchwork presence, beautifully bright!

**Chasing Thoughts Lost in the Wind**


Thoughts scatter like leaves in the breeze,
Attempting to catch them, oh what a tease!
They flutter and flip, with laughter they spin,
"Methinks you're not catching," they cheekily grin.

I follow a thought that floats by with flair,
Only to find it's just empty air.
"Where have you gone?" I shout to the sky,
But all I receive is a question mark's sigh.

I trip on a notion that seems quite profound,
Only to land with a bounce on the ground.
Now with each chase, I just shake my head,
These whimsical musings could fill me with dread!

Yet, giggles erupt as I run to and fro,
For in every slip, there's a certain glow.
So I'll bound after whims like a child at play,
In this breezy dance, I'll find my way!

## **Unraveled yarns of Existence**

With each strand I tug, the yarn starts to fray,
Pulling a thread, and it leads me astray.
Questions and answers all tangled in knots,
I stitch my thoughts like crazy robots.

Once a straight line, now a jumbled mess,
I laugh at the chaos, I must confess.
Who knew that these fibers could weave such delight?
In the fabric of life, I'm afraid of the night.

So I tie my shoes, and off I prance,
Dancing with destiny, giving it a chance.
At the end of my thread, I find a bright twirl,
Saying "What a ride!" as it starts to unfurl.

In the tapestry's whimsy, the fun truly lies,
Each loop tells a tale, and the laughter just flies.
So I embrace every knot, every twist, every turn,
In this yarn of existence, there's always more to learn!

## The Symphony of Solitude

In a room where the echoes play,
A sock on the floor leads the ballet.
The chair and the fridge have a chat,
While the dust bunnies dance, imagine that!

The clock ticks slowly, time's not a friend,
Maybe it's ramen I need to transcend.
With a smile, I ponder this life's little quirks,
In my solo orchestra where boredom lurks.

The cat on the windowsill, so wise,
Judges my choices with her bright eyes.
As I wear mismatched socks with glee,
Who knew solitude could be such a spree?

So I tip my hat to the silence around,
And to my imaginary band, I'm bound.
Life is a concert, my quirks take the lead,
Laughing at absurdities, that's all I need!

**Chasing Illumination**


With a flashlight in hand, I roam at night,
Chasing shadows, seeking the light.
The bugs come dancing, find them quite keen,
Turns out they're just critters in search of a scene!

A map full of stars, oh what a joke,
Every turn leads me to another folk.
"Where's enlightenment?" I ask the moon,
She giggles and says, "You'll find it real soon!"

The GPS recalculates, what a blunder,
I'm lost in the cosmos, oh what a wonder!
Wearing mismatched shoes, I tiptoe on air,
Illuminated by laughter, swirling everywhere.

So I dance with the fireflies, sing with the trees,
Chasing that glow with careless ease.
Maybe the light's not a thing we chase,
But a silly dance, a joyous embrace!

## Mosaic of a Nameless Journey

Collecting odd pieces, a life-like art,
A fork in the road, now that's a start.
Socks with holes tell tales of their own,
Woven together, this chaos I've grown.

A spoon thinks it's fancy, a gold-plated prize,
While the plate just rolls its unbothered eyes.
With each little detour, I find my delight,
Like a jigsaw puzzle that's missing the light.

Road trips with snacks and songs that skew,
Navigating life like it's a zoo.
Each moment's a canvas, a splash of pure fun,
I laugh through the colors, oh I'm never done!

So here's to the mess, to the playful array,
Life's stitched together in a whimsical way.
With each piece I hold, I just have to grin,
This mosaic of chaos, let the fun begin!

## The Mapless Expedition

Off we go without a clue in sight,
On a quest with laughter, feeling quite light.
With pockets of snacks and a questionable plan,
Who needs a map when you have a whimsy span?

The compass spins wildly, what a delight,
"Right or is it left?"—we'll know by tonight.
Each twist of the road leads us to cheer,
With every wrong turn, adventure draws near.

From mishaps with llamas to ice cream galore,
A journey uncharted, oh we want more!
With flip-flops and hats, we waddle along,
Creating new tales, our spirits are strong.

So here's to the wanderers, lost in the fun,
With laughter and joy, we'll never be done.
For life's map is blank, let's color outside,
Embrace the absurd and enjoy the ride!

## The Spectrum of Awareness

In a world that spins like a top,
We chase our tails and never stop.
With wisdom wrapped in boxes small,
We smile and say, 'I've got it all!'

But boxes leak and packages fall,
What's quirky yonder? That's the call!
We juggle thoughts, unsure, confused,
While sipping tea, feeling bemused.

The colors fade and blend like paint,
As we debate what makes us quaint.
With every hiccup, laugh, and sigh,
We find our truths, then wave goodbye!

Oh, the spectrum gives a wink and smile,
As we ponder for a little while.
Bubble wrap, our joyful friend,
In this dance that has no end!

## An Endless Scroll of Possibilities

Scrolling down the cosmic feed,
In search of answers, yes indeed!
A meme that says, 'Just chill out, dude,'
May hold wise secrets wrapped in crude.

Each swipe reveals a quirky scene,
A cat in pants, a carrot queen.
We ponder life, the vast array,
While laughing hard, we lose our way.

'Next video,' we click without a care,
Chasing wisdom that's almost there.
But looped in fun, we find our bliss,
In silly gifs, we reminisce.

So pause and breathe, don't miss the chance,
To find your truth in the wild dance.
For scrolling through, we laugh out loud,
In this circus, we're all so proud!

## Ripples in the Fabric of Time

Time's a river, flows like a stream,
With splashy giggles, life's a dream.
A pebble tossed, a ripple spins,
And laughter echoes where it begins.

We ponder fate like laundry hung,
'Is that my fate or just a pun?'
The fabric twists, a curious sight,
Stitching together the day and night.

In denim days and twinkly stars,
We find our truths in life's bizarre.
With patterns woven, some a mess,
We wear confusion like a dress.

Oh, ripples tingle, make us grin,
As we chase moments with a spin.
Pocket the laughter, it fits just right—
In time's grand dance, we take our flight!

## The Intelligence of the Unanswerable

Questions bounce like crazy balls,
'Why are we here?' the clarion calls.
With every riddle, we laugh and sigh,
While pondering clouds drifting by.

One thought leads to another wild chase,
Like socks that vanish, intertwining space.
Wisdom's a puzzle, pieces askew,
Wrapped in a riddle, what to do?

Tick-tock goes the clock on the wall,
We chase the thoughts, we stumble, we fall.
But giggles rise where answers hide,
In the ruckus, joy cannot abide.

So indulge in the whimsy, roll with the fun,
For questions make life an endless run.
In laughter's embrace, we find our way,
Through the unanswerable, come what may!

## The Quest Beyond Labels

We search for tags that fit us well,
But labels stick like gum to shoe.
Life's an unwrapped gift, can't you tell?
With no instruction manual in view.

Trying to be what others say,
Like a cat that wants to bark and bite,
We stumble through each silly day,
Wearing socks that never match quite right.

What's your title, what's your role?
An artist? Chef? The world's a stage!
Maybe we're just a rocking soul,
Dancing through each awkward page.

So let's embrace this quirky pie,
With each odd slice, we take a bite.
We'll laugh until we almost cry,
And find the joy in all that's light.

## Uncharted Horizons

We sail on seas of endless thought,
With maps that squiggle all around.
Ahoy, what treasures have we sought?
Just crab cakes and laughs we found!

Navigating through the unknown,
Our compass spins in dizzy glee.
Do parrots talk? Is it just tone?
Does anyone know the key to be?

Each wave a joke, each breeze a pun,
We'll ride the surf of life's delight.
With every splash, the silliness spun,
As the sun sets on our laughter-filled night.

So hoist the sails and chase the fun,
For life's a boat with room to roam.
Let's drink the sea until we're done,
And make each wave our wobbly home.

## The Paradox of Purpose

Chasing purpose like a wild hare,
We end up in circles, round and round.
Is it the chase, or is it fair?
With every leap, a new absurdity found.

Work hard, they say, find what you live,
But donuts speak wisdom, glazed and sweet.
The more you seek, the less you give,
As life giggles at your stubborn feat.

Is it in toil or in quirky art?
The universe shrugs with playful cheer.
Just when you think you know your part,
The cat leaps in, and all is unclear!

So let's uncork joy and take a sip,
Dance on the chaos, without a care.
For in this dance, the paradox trips,
And laughter's the purpose we all can share.

## In Search of Lost Joy

I searched for joy in all the nooks,
Under cushions and in old shoes.
Yet all I found were dusty books,
   And recipes I couldn't use.

Like seeking socks that never mate,
I chased it down the pants of fate.
In clowns and pies, I thought I'd see,
But joy was hiding, snickering at me.

With every frown, I spun around,
Found my laughter stuck in a jar.
The more I searched, the less I found,
   Until I hit my funny bone hard.

So I tossed the map, forgot the quest,
And laughed at life, my closest friend.
For joy's not found, just like a jest,
   It dances close, around each bend.

## Unveiling the Essence

In a world of shiny gadgets,
We search for the golden key.
Wrapped in life's gift package,
They forgot to send the manual for me.

Chasing dreams like a puppy,
Tangled in a ball of yarn.
Dancing to tunes all bumpy,
While tripping on our own charm.

Cereal box wisdom, I swear,
Offers tips on success.
"Add milk and a little flair,"
But fails to deal with the stress.

So we laugh through the unknown,
With humor as our guide.
Life's a silly little drone,
Taking us for a wild ride.

# The Journey Without Instructions

With no map to trace or follow,
We wander without a plan.
Hoping life will fill the hollow,
Like a quirky, lost caravan.

Each twist reveals a surprise,
Like stepping on a hidden bee.
Unexpected gifts in disguise,
Giggling at what's yet to be!

We skip along this wacky trail,
Stumbling over our own feet.
In laughing circles, we prevail,
As we face life's tasty treat.

So here's to the clueless ride,
Where instructions are a myth.
Joy's the compass, come what tide,
With each belly laugh, a gift!

**Fragments of Fulfillment**


Life's a jigsaw, odd and great,
Pieces scattered everywhere.
Trying hard to set the state,
But the cat stole my favorite square!

Happiness in cereal boxes,
And socks that never match.
Finding joy in tiny foxes,
And pictures of my mom's mustache.

Searching for the missing piece,
We giggle in our chase.
Each misfit holds a slice of peace,
In this funny, crazy race.

Every bump, a step that shows,
Life's way of making art.
In swirls of laughter, joy just grows,
And we learn to play the part!

## Moments in an Empty Box

Open it up, what do I see?
Nothing but a shiny glare.
An empty box that's laughing at me,
With jokes floating in the air.

I ponder on this vacuous space,
Expecting treasures galore.
Turns out, it's just a funny face,
Reminding me there's always more!

Each moment spent in this void,
Is filled with laughter and cheer.
Life's humor can't be destroyed,
Even when there's nothing near.

So I dance with the empty air,
And twirl in this playful game.
The joy's not in what's "not there,"
But in laughter's wild acclaim!

## Footprints in a Timeless Desert

In the sands, I leave my mark,
But the wind just laughs and sparks.
Mirages dance, they tease my sight,
Always shifting, day to night.

With each step, I ponder round,
Why the ground has no solid sound.
Camel rides, they flop and sway,
Yet here I am, lost on my way.

Under stars, I take a seat,
Count the grains beneath my feet.
"Where to next?" I shout and grin,
As a tumbleweed rolls in with a spin.

In this vast, absurd expanse,
I keep on laughing at the chance.
Life's a joke, a quirky jest,
With empty pockets, I feel blessed.

## The Ocean of Unanswered Questions

I dipped my toes in thought today,
Caught a wave of, 'What'll they say?'
The fish just stared, the crabs held court,
While seagulls squawked from their floaty fort.

"Why are we here?" the jellyfish asked,
And with a flap, my thoughts were tasked.
They swayed and laughed in salty glee,
Not a clue what's next for me!

Treasure chests of questions, wide,
But no map, just a bumpy ride.
I surfed on doubt, caught a big bite,
As the sun sank low, blue turned to night.

With a splash and giggle, I swim back in,
Because overthinking's where all jokes begin.
So with sand in my hair, I shout to the sea,
"Who needs answers when you're just so free?"

## Conversations with the Infinite

I called up space, just for a chat,
"Is all this real?" I asked the cat.
Sipping stars from a cosmic cup,
The answers got too heavy to sup.

Distant galaxies wink and tease,
While I'm stuck down here, scratching my knees.
"Hey, universe, what's the scoop?"
It giggled back, "Just join the loop!"

Time's a jester with endless puns,
I tried to catch it, but it runs.
"Am I the punchline?" I start to fret,
But the cosmos just chuckles, "Not quite yet!"

So I sit and spin on this tiny sphere,
With quirky quirks that bring good cheer.
In this strange banter, I find my role,
A fool in a play, but hey, that's the goal!

## The Essence of Empty Spaces

In the corners where dust bunnies play,
I find my thoughts in a funny ballet.
Each blank wall holds a silly grin,
As echoes chat and let the fun begin.

Here's a sock, there's a shoe,
Twirling with dreams, who knew?
I poke at the void with a rubber chicken,
In this silence, laughter's kickin'.

An empty chair for a missing friend,
"Join me in giggles," I happily send.
Philosophers hide in my coffee cup,
While I sip the absurd, I feel tied up!

So here's to spaces that speak such glee,
To the nonsense that dances, wild and free.
In emptiness, I find delight,
A paradox wrapped in giggles, so bright.

**The Unwrapped Gift**

A box so wide, no bow in sight,
Inside it shimmers, oh what a fright!
Unraveled dreams, here on display,
Instructions missing, lost in the fray.

Who needs a manual, or a guide?
We twist and turn, with pride as our ride.
Let's play a game, a riddle or two,
What's fun about life, if unwrapped, it's blue!

The ribbons dance, we giggle and cheer,
As we unwrap laughter while munching on beer.
Uncertain terrain, it's quite the show,
Jump in, my friend, let's go with the flow!

Here's a spark, let's light the night,
With a peek inside, it's quite the sight!
So laugh with me, let fate take a spin,
This gift of a ride is where we begin!

## Echoes of Existence

In the hall of echoes, footsteps of glee,
A yawn of the cosmos, sings 'how to be!'
With hiccups and chuckles, life wears a grin,
A jester's parade, let the fun begin!

A dance on the edge, twirls of delight,
As we search for the twinkle in endless night.
Is it deep? Is it shallow? A riddle so bold,
The answer is laughter—just watch it unfold!

Awake in a swirl, lost in routine,
Stumbling through chaos, a slapstick scene.
Whispers of wisdom, wrapped in a jest,
Echoes remind us, to seek out the best!

Through ups and downs, we juggle the fate,
With a wink to the night, we dance with the great.
So step to the rhythm, join in the play,
This echo of laughter, don't let it stray!

## **Threads of Purpose**

A tangle of yarn, colorfully spun,
Weaving our stories, oh what fun!
Knots of confusion, frayed at the seam,
But each twist and turn is part of the dream.

The needle darts quick, threading the light,
Creating a tapestry, day and night.
With each stumble, a stitch so neat,
We laugh as we trip on our own two feet!

Purpose is quirky, a jest in disguise,
With patterns of joy, this we surmise.
So bring out the thread and let's make it bold,
Life's fabric is funny, more precious than gold!

So gather the colors, paint with a grin,
The loom of existence, weaves thick and thin.
Let laughter be the thread, bright and warm,
In a fabric of joy, we'll weather the storm!

## Navigating the Void

A boat made of laughter, floats in the air,
With giggles for sails, we glide without care.
The map's upside down, but who needs a chart?
We'll steer through the void, with a merry heart!

What lies in the depths? A mystery to seek,
With shadows and echoes, we play hide-and-seek.
The stars throw a party, they twinkle and shout,
As we sail through the cosmos without a doubt!

Quirky encounters, dolphins that sing,
Waves of wild wonders, oh, what joy they bring!
Navigating the void, in a rickety craft,
Life's joys are the compass that steer our laugh!

So hoist up the sails, let's ride the night tide,
A voyage of fun, with laughter as guide.
Through voids and through dreams, we'll dance and rejoice,
In this mad little journey, let's treasure our choice!

## The Here and Now of Exploration

In search of answers, we all roam,
Lost in the quest to find a home.
With maps that lead to nowhere fast,
We trudge along, we laugh, we gasp.

A fortune cookie, what does it say?
"Find joy in chaos, come what may!"
We dance on roads both long and wide,
With each wrong turn, a giggling ride.

Around the bend, a sign appears,
"The truth is here!" it grins and cheers.
Yet still we ponder, minds in whirl,
Life's just a joke, not a pearl.

So let us sip from cups of glee,
As we invent our own decree.
With silly hats and hearts so bold,
We navigate this world of gold.

## Over the Edge of Understanding

Peering over this abyss we think,
With questions hanging on the brink.
Is there a net, or do we fall?
Perhaps it's jello! Who can call?

We juggle dreams, we flip and glide,
In this circus of the mind, we ride.
A unicycle or maybe shoes?
Who needs straight paths when we choose to cruise?

Philosophers nod and scratch their heads,
While we sip soda from our beds.
Their wisdom's vast, yet ours is fun,
A giggle shared beats a loaded gun.

So toast to the questions that never cease,
In the chaos, we find our peace.
With every tumble, laugh it off,
The journey's rich with every scoff.

## Hues of a Distant Tomorrow

Tomorrow's colors, oh what a sight,
Dancing with dreams in broad daylight.
We throw our fears like old confetti,
Wearing absurd hats, feeling ready.

Will it be green, or perhaps a blue?
We sketch our futures with crayons too.
Each line a promise, a scribbled grind,
Life's abstract art, oh how it twines!

The canvas stretches, colors collide,
With every splash, we take a ride.
Gaussian curves and wavy shapes,
More fun than math, oh what escapes!

So paint your day with giggles bold,
And find the joy in tales retold.
In hues of rainbows, dance and play,
Tomorrow's bright—just seize the day!

## In the Footnotes of Existence

In margins where the scribbles lie,
We find the truths that tickle by.
With footnotes deep as oceans wide,
We laugh at thoughts we tried to hide.

"Turn the page," a wise man said,
As we munch snacks and scratch our head.
Philosophy with popcorn's best,
As laughter reigns and thoughts digress.

A footnote here, a tangent there,
We chase our tails without a care.
These tiny notes hold mighty tales,
Like kittens lost in grand old gales.

So let's be silly, flip the script,
In life's great book, we're underscripted.
Amidst the jokes and playful spins,
The heart of life's where fun begins!

## **Searching for Significance**

In a world full of stuff, where do we begin,
Searching for the joy, amidst the din?
Do we find it in snacks, or maybe in tea?
Or is it just hiding behind the TV?

I checked all the boxes, still feeling lost,
Counting my pennies, but oh, the cost!
I tried to be deep, but fell in the pool,
Life's just a game, and I'm missing the rules.

With every new gadget, they say I will grow,
But I'm still just a kid in an adult's show.
Should I chase all the trends, or dance in the rain?
Or play with my socks and go a bit insane?

Perhaps the secret's in laughter and cake,
A slice of delight, for goodness' sake!
I ponder my fate with a smirk on my face,
Maybe the point is just keeping up pace.

# Unboxed Dreams

I got a big package labeled 'What's Your Goal?'
Tore it open quickly, lost control of my soul.
Inside was a mirror, a pair of old shoes,
And a note that just said, 'You've got nothing to lose.'

I dusted off dreams that I lost in the fray,
Like toys in the attic, waiting for play.
In this cosmic store, will I find the right toy?
A humor-filled life, please sprinkle with joy!

With each silly misstep, I stumble and laugh,
Is there an instruction manual? Maybe a graph?
I'll take what I get, and dance through the day,
Life's just a dance floor, come join in the sway.

Unboxed dreams still rattle as I prance around,
Who needs a map when silliness is found?
Forget all the 'rules,' let the fun unfold,
In this whimsical journey, be daring and bold.

## The Puzzle of Being

I've got a jigsaw with pieces to spare,
But the corners are missing, not one is a pair.
I try to connect them, they laugh and fly free,
This puzzle of being is puzzling to me.

The box says 'Fulfillment', but what does it mean?
Those pieces just giggle, not fitting the scene.
Do I force them together with tape and some glue?
Or hop on a unicorn and chase down the blue?

I tried stacking values like pancakes so tall,
But each bite I take just leads to a fall.
Maybe they're meant to be scattered around,
Like confetti of choice, in a vibrant sound.

With quirks and the chaos, I'll dance through the strife,
Embrace all the nonsense, that's the spice of life!
So here's to the riddles, the giggles, the pain,
Life's greatest puzzle is joy in the rain.

## Whispers in the Wilderness

In the wilds of my mind, there's chatter galore,
Whispers of wisdom, but what's behind door four?
I chase down the shadows, they tickle my thoughts,
Finding humor in rabbits who dance in their spots.

There's magic in stardust, a hint from the breeze,
But did I just eat that? Oh, please pass the peas!
The universe giggles, in stars that collide,
Life's just a circus; can I join in the ride?

Philosophy's wild, and I'm swaying with trees,
Who knew I'd find answers in bumblebee bees?
Twirling in circles, let laughter ensue,
The secrets we seek are hidden in the goo.

So I'll wander these woods, with a grin on my face,
Embracing the chaos, finding my place.
With whispers of joy in this wilderness roam,
Creating a life that feels just like home.

## Whispers in the Void

In the attic of my brain,
Dust-mites dance and spin,
They whisper secrets we can't gain,
As laughter draws me in.

A squirrel wearing glasses looks,
At charts of how to thrive,
He furrows brow, rereads old books,
Decides to nap instead of strive.

The clock's hand's ticking like a drum,
Each tick a question mark,
When did my life become so glum?
Oh wait, it's just a lark!

I chase my tail like a confused dog,
Thinking maybe that's the point,
In a world like this, full of fog,
I'll party at the joint!

## Beyond the Horizon of Understanding

They say love makes the world go round,
But I'm stuck on a seesaw,
With my snacks strewn on the ground,
And my dog just gave me a paw.

The sun is bright, the grass is green,
Yet questions bounce like a ball,
Where's the manual, could it be seen?
If only I could recall!

A philosopher on a soapbox shouts,
'The sky is blue, and so are we!'
I nod along, ignoring the doubts,
While sipping a fizzy freebie.

Oh, the wonders of cosmic jest,
Are we really all just jokes?
In a universe that's quite a mess,
I'll join the fun and poke!

## The Journey's Intricate Map

With crumbs of thought strewn like a trail,
I wander through life's maze,
A map unfolded, but full of fail,
My sense of direction sways.

A compass spins like a top,
Pointing to some grand reveal,
But all I find is a soda shop,
Of plastic seats and a meal.

I ask a monkey for some aid,
He pulls a banana from his cheek,
"Follow your heart," he quaintly said,
But I'm still feeling quite weak.

Yet laughter echoes in my chest,
As I trip over my shoes,
It looks like joy is quite the guest,
In this delightful ruse!

# Life's Catalog of Uncertainties

I flipped through the catalog of fate,
But all I found was a sock,
Some lucky charms, and a heavy crate,
Filled with memories that mock.

"Return it if you feel misplaced,"
The fine print danced with glee,
As if to say, in life's wild race,
The joke is just to be free!

I've tried bubbling potions and rhymes,
To navigate this swirling craft,
Yet still I dance through random climes,
With laughter as my gift and craft.

So here's to doubts, to joys unforeseen,
To socks that never find their pair,
In life's great show, be bold and keen,
For fun is found everywhere!

www.ingramcontent.com/pod-product-compliance
Lightning Source LLC
Chambersburg PA
CBHW051638160426
43209CB00004B/703